P9-BZF-051

Flowers That Never Fade

FLOWERS THAT NEVER FADE

Copyright 1959, 1990, Leroy Brownlow
Brownlow Publishing Company, Inc.
6309 Airport Freeway,
Fort Worth, Texas 76117

◆

All rights reserved. The use or reprinting
of any part of this book without the express written
permission of the publisher is prohibited.
ISBN: 0-915720-00-0

A Gift For

JoAnn

From

Carolyn

Dec. 19 99

◆

Brownlow Gift Books

A Few Hallelujahs for Your Ho-Hums
A Psalm in My Heart
Angels of Mercy, Whispers of Love
As a Man Thinketh
Cheerful Hearts
Children Won't Wait
Flowers for Mother
Flowers for You
Flowers of Friendship
Flowers That Never Fade
For Mom With Love
Gardens of the Heart
Give Us This Day
Grandpa Was a Preacher
Jesus Wept
Just Between Friends
Leaves of Gold
Let's Laugh a Little
Love Is Forever
Making the Most of Life
The Greatest Thing in the World
Thoughts of Gold—Wisdom for Living
Today and Forever
Today Is Mine
University of Hard Knocks
Your Special Day

Flowers That Never Fade

Leroy Brownlow

Words of Hope
and Inspiration
With Everlasting Value

BROWNLOW PUBLISHING COMPANY, INC.
FORT WORTH, TEXAS

Contents

CHAPTER ONE

A Light Unto My Path

The Psalmist said, "Thy word is a lamp unto my feet, and a light unto my path" (Psalms 119:105). The Bible is God's book of light to a world dark and destitute of knowledge. It sheds light on our origin, duty, and destiny. It tells us from whence we come, how to live, and where we are going. It tells us how to live with ourselves, with our fellowmen, and with God. It is a foundation for our feet, a map for our eyes, a sword for our hands, food for our souls, and a healing balm for our hearts.

The secrets of successful living are unfolded in its pages. The light in human books had its origin in the one great book, the Bible. It is the lamp from which all other lights receive their rays. There is a divinity about it that makes it shine among books

like the diamond glistens among stones. It is the Heavenly Father's gracious book of counsel and consolation to His children here on earth.

• *The idea of a divine source book of light to a benighted race is reasonable.* Our world is filled with the darkness of sin and suffering, disappointment and despair, heartache and helplessness. In the darkness of the night, man's every impulse cries out for light that this world cannot furnish. His weakness and weariness, his suffering and sorrow, his ambition and anguish, truly indicate that man has more than an animal capacity for living. It is unreasonable to assume that such aspirations for guidance and comfort would exist in the soul only to perish forever in this life.

The undeveloped powers of the soul and the yearnings of the human heart demand a divine revelation which furnishes to us the help and strength of a Higher Power. If God exists— and He does— it is intelligent to assume that He would communicate with us, His needy offspring, in some definite and concrete manner— hence, the Bible. It is absolutely preposterous to think that God would create man and place him in a dark, chaotic world with no light for his path and no hope for his heart. So the idea of the Divine Book is just as reasonable as the idea of the Divine Being.

• *The Bible claims to be God's inspired book* which fills our needs. It says, "All Scripture is given by inspiration of God, and is profitable for doctrine, for reproof, for correction, for instruction in righteousness: that the man of God may be perfect, thoroughly furnished unto all good works" (II Timothy 3:16-17). It is God's book of science on right living.

"By their fruits ye shall know them" is a challenging and discriminative test. Good fruit does not come from a corrupt tree. Neither does pure water flow from a spring of poison. The Bible has always produced good fruit; therefore, it must be a good book. This is why it graces almost every home in the land, why it is the staff of a million pilgrims passing through this world, why its comfort has been on the lips of an innumerable host as they walked through the valley of the shadow of death, and why its words stand engraved today upon ten thousand marble markers in the silent cities of the dead. Why? It is heaven's message to earth's people.

• *The Bible has been criticized, tested,* and weighed in the balance, but not a one of its truths has failed, nor one ray of its light grown dimmer. Nations have perished, customs have been altered, and manners have changed. But age has failed to weaken its power.

The enemies of the Bible perished and have soon been forgotten one after another, but the Bible keeps on living.

◆

*Tradition has dug for it a grave, intolerance
has lighted for it many a fagot, many a Judas
has betrayed it with a kiss, many a Peter has
denied it with an oath, many a Demas has
forsaken it; but the word of God still endures.*

• *There is no other book comparable to the
Bible.* It contains the choicest gems of thought, the
wisest instruction, the highest code of morality, the
sweetest comfort, coupled with a rareness and a
richness unknown to any other book.

Christ's Sermon on the Mount is the greatest
and sublimest code of morals to be found on this
earth (Matthew 5-7). It has been called the Magna
Charta of Christ's Kingdom. There is in the sermon
a beauty of words, a directness of thought, a brevi-
ty of instruction, and a simplicity of expression
unlike any other sermon ever preached.

Christ's Parable of the Prodigal Son is recog-
nized as one of the classic stories in literature. It
is regarded as the pearl of parables. It has been
precious to all classes and ages of people on every
shore and in every clime. It excels all human works
of fiction in its portrayal of character. The tenderness of that father has helped millions to better
understand and appreciate God's love for sinful
man.

And what loveliness of devotion and true
fidelity are found in the words of Ruth:

◆

Entreat me not to leave thee,
Or to return from following after thee:
For whither thou goest, I will go;
And where thou lodgest, I will lodge:
Thy people shall be my people,
And thy God my God.
Where thou diest, will I die,
And there will I be buried:
The Lord do so to me, and more also,
If aught but death part thee and me.

—RUTH 1:16,17

Even Voltaire said the Book of Ruth "was beyond anything found in Homer or in any other classic writers."

If you would like to weigh logic, then read Hebrews or study Paul's sermon on Mars Hill, found in Acts. Or if you would like to ponder wise sayings and meditate upon maxims, then turn to the Book of Proverbs. There is nothing in human literature in this field that even begins to approach it.

Words, verses, and volumes have been written on the romantic subject of love. But the Bible's definition of love outshines all human sayings on this heart-warming theme:

Love suffereth long, and is kind;
Love envieth not; love vaunteth not itself,

◆

Is not puffed up, doth not behave itself
   unseemly,
Seeketh not its own, is not provoked,
Taketh not account of evil;
Rejoiceth not in unrighteousness,
But rejoiceth with the truth;
Beareth all things, believeth all things,
Hopeth all things, endureth all things.
Love never faileth.

—I CORINTHIANS 13
American Standard
Version

If you are sad and lonely, if your heart is struck with fear and you feel the need of strength and guidance, then read the immortal Twenty-third Psalm, given by the Hebrew shepherd boy; for it is a Gibraltar in both life and death:

The Lord is my shepherd;
I shall not want.
He maketh me to lie down in green pastures:
He leadeth me beside the still waters.
He restoreth my soul:
He leadeth me in the paths of righteousness
   for his name's sake.
Yea, though I walk through the valley
   of the shadow of death,
I will fear no evil:

◆

For thou art with me;
Thy rod and thy staff they comfort me.
Thou preparest a table before me
    in the presence of mine enemies:
Thou anointest my head with oil;
My cup runneth over.
Surely goodness and mercy shall follow me
    all the days of my life:
And I will dwell in the house of the Lord
    forever.

This is only a sample and a tiny part of what is found in the Holy Bible. We would not think of finding in the works of Aristotle and Plato such guidance for the feet, such strength for the hands, such sweetness for personality, and such hope for the heart. This is why the lessons to follow in this book will be based upon the truths and principles of successful and happy living first given in the Bible. It is the key that unlocks our problems.

CHAPTER TWO

This Troubled World

No life is wholly exempt from suffering and distress. This has been true of man since the day Adam and Eve fell and were driven from the Garden of Eden. That was the day God said to man, "Cursed is the ground for thy sake; in sorrow shalt thou eat of it all the days of thy life" (Genesis 3:17). Not being able to look into the hearts of those around us, we think them fortunate and free from trouble, because we can only see the superficial signs of prosperity and success. But every heart knows its own suffering.

• *Anxieties touch both the young and the old.* Trouble is no respecter of age. The young sometimes imagine that time will cure all their problems, while the aged sometimes look at youth and think them trouble-free. Problems vary with age, but every age has its own troubles and every heart

◆

knows its own care.

Even little children have blows to fall upon them with a mighty impact. We think their problems are only childish, but to them they are severe and trying.

The perplexities of youth are so acute. They are faced with basic decisions that affect their entire future. They are so young and inexperienced to have to make such major decisions. Oftentimes their hearts break, and older ones do not understand. They have care enough to distress any heart. They need the sympathetic help of those who have lived longer and have been over the road.

Those in middle-age also have their problems. They stand at the noon-day hour of life. They are passing from morning to the evening in life's little day. This brings certain difficulties and disappointments which are peculiar to this age. Adjustments are necessary for them to live happily.

The older ones have their cares too. They have come a long way in the road of life, but they have never been able to get completely away from troubles.

So persons in every age group need help, strength, and encouragement.

• *Trouble comes to the rich and poor.* Ill winds blow against all homes. Wealth is no bar against troubles; often it serves only as a magnet which draws them. Trouble respects no one's person, fortune, or rank. Disappointment and dismay, anguish and agony, sickness and death enter alike the

◆

homes of the rich and the poor, the exalted and the humble, the learned and the illiterate. Heavy hangs many a head that wears a crown. In many a mansion there abides an ever-consuming sorrow hidden and unknown to the public. Fame, wealth, and other symbols of success often do little more than veil the sorrows of the heart.

• *Distress comes to the wicked.* They seek the pleasures of the world, but trouble always overtakes them. The fascinating allurements and the enticing amusements of sin increase man's troubles rather than diminish them. The wise man Solomon laid down this principle of life: "Remember now thy Creator in the days of thy youth, while the evil days come not, nor the years draw nigh, when thou shalt say, I have no pleasure in them" (Ecclesiastes 12:1). Sin is a thief that steals the joy from a world that already has too little of it.

• *Disturbance comes to the righteous.* Paul was one of the best men of all ages, but trouble followed him like a shadow. He suffered affliction and persecution more than many others of his day— he even died a martyr's death. But he learned to suffer gracefully and to profit from adverse experiences. He knew that it took contrary winds to lift the kite and that there would be no rainbows if there were no clouds. He saw his sufferings as blessings in disguise. He wrote, "But I would ye should understand, brethren, that the things which happened unto me have fallen out rather unto the furtherance of the gospel" (Philippians 1:12). He found refuge in his distresses. He found the secret of dealing with life's unpleasantries. Hence, he wrote, "I have learned, in whatsoever state I am, therewith to be content" (Philippians 4:11). For him, this took the poison out of life's cruel bite.

There is no mistake about it — this earth is not heaven. The pathway of life is crowded with sorrows. But every traveler may so walk as to enter the land where sorrows are unknown.

The path of sorrow and that path alone
Leads to the land where sorrow is unknown.
No traveler ever reached this blest abode
Who found not thorns and briers in his road.

— WILLIAM COWPER

CHAPTER THREE

Strength to Endure Suffering

*T*here are many kinds of suffering— physical pain, mental anxiety, bereavement, and a world of others. But regardless of the kind, our calamity is God's opportunity.

• *Belief in God as a refuge and a present help strengthens the sufferer.* Faith in God turns our dark clouds into sunshine, because we believe this precious truth: "But my God shall supply all your need according to his riches in glory by Christ Jesus" (Philippians 4:19). Needs! Needs! A thousand needs! And God shall supply all of them. Supply not what we may want, but what we need.

> *Before me, even as behind,*
> *God is — and all is well.*

— JOHN GREENLEAF WHITTIER

❖

Faith in God strengthened the writer of Psalms when he was almost at the fainting point. He said, "I had fainted, unless I had believed to see the goodness of the Lord in the land of the living" (Psalms 27:13). He had experienced a close call. But at the height of the crisis, faith lifted him up and gave him strength. If we draw nigh to God, He will draw nigh to us, and any person close to God is never far from help.

Though destruction walk around us,
Though the arrows past us fly,
Angel-guards from Thee surround us;
We are safe if Thou art nigh.

— AUTHOR UNKNOWN

• *In our distress we find the capacity for endurance through prayer to God.* David said, "In my distress I cried unto the Lord, and he heard me" (Psalms 120:1) In the hour of ease we may think we can get along without God. Of course, we cannot; we just think so. But in the hour of distress when the help of man fails us, then up goes our cry to the Father, because there is no fear the heavenly Father cannot quiet, and there is no heartache He cannot cure.

Sometimes God answers our prayers with a complete deliverance from distress, and sometimes with a modification of that agony, and at other

◆

times by granting blessings whereby we are able to bear it patiently. God does not always answer our prayers by giving us exactly what we ask. He loves us too much for this. Instead, He gives us what is best for us.

Many have used prayer; many others have abused it. Not all who pray are heard. "Ye ask, and receive not" (James 4:3). Why? Because acceptable prayer is a conditional thing. The conditions demand that we be righteous, obedient, forgiving, a person of faith, pray in harmony with God's will, and pray in Jesus' name. This kind of praying is effectual; it is more than relief from pent-up tensions; it is the connecting line to the throne of God.

Amidst all dangers, afflictions, and embarrassments, many have experienced through prayer the calmness, tranquility, and sweetness of life promised in this passage: "Be careful for nothing [In nothing be anxious, A.S.V.]; but in everything by prayer and supplication with thanksgiving let your requests be made known unto God. And the peace of God, which passeth all understanding, shall keep your hearts and minds through Christ Jesus" (Philippians 4:6,7).

• *God's gracious providence affords courage to all who love the Lord.* The Bible says, "And we know that all things work together for good to them that love God, to them who are called accord-

◆

ing to his purpose" (Romans 8:28). The adversities of life will be overruled by the almighty and wise God to produce the eternal and permanent good of those who love the Lord. This promise gives us strength for every eventuality.

Trials and afflictions teach us the truth about our transitory condition, and take our affections from this world and center them on things eternal. They produce a subdued patience, a humble temper, and a kind disposition. However, adversities often have the opposite effect upon sinners. They are hardened by their refusal to submit to the obvious design of suffering. But the Christian in his suffering, like Job of old, sins not nor charges God foolishly (Job 1:22). He understands that chastisement is for his good (Hebrews 12:5-11).

Even though adversities and trials have never seemed good at the time, all saints have seen their value; and toward the end of life have said that it was good for them to have been afflicted. David said, "Before I was afflicted I went astray: but now have I kept thy word... It is good for me that I have been afflicted; that I might learn thy statutes" (Psalms 119:67-71).

Out of our human weaknesses, there may come moments when we are tempted to doubt that all things are working for our good. This is due to our shortsightedness. We are tempted to think in the limited terms of the present and to appraise in the

◆

narrow scope of what we presently feel and see. Though our trials and afflictions are numerous and long-endured, we know from God's revelation and from our own experiences that they work for our good — that is, if we love God. For this is a conditional promise — "to them that love God." And Jesus said, "If a man love me, he will keep my words" (John 14:23). If we comply with the condition, God will keep the promise.

> *My life is but a weaving between my Lord*
>   *and me;*
> *I may not choose the colors, He knows what*
>   *they should be;*
> *For He can view the pattern upon the upper*
>   *side,*
> *While I can see it only on this, the under side.*
> *Sometimes He weaveth sorrow, which seemeth*
>   *strange to me;*
> *But I will trust His judgment and work on*
>   *faithfully;*
> *'Tis He who fills the shuttle, He knows just*
>   *what is best;*
> *So I shall weave in earnest and leave with*
>   *Him the rest.*
> *Not till the loom is silent and the shuttles*
>   *cease to fly,*

◆

*Shall God unroll the canvas and explain the
   reason why —
The dark threads are as needful in the
   Weaver's skillful hand
As the threads of gold and silver in the pattern
   He has planned.
He knows, He loves, He cares. Nothing this
   truth can dim.
He gives His very best to those who leave the
   choice to Him.*

— JOHN BANNISTER

• *We may obtain rest from our burdens by simply casting them on the Lord.* David said, "Cast thy
burden upon the Lord, and he shall sustain thee"
(Psalms 55:22). And Peter said, "Casting all your
care upon him; for he careth for you" (I Peter 5:7).
The weight of life's cares and sufferings are too
burdensome for us to try to carry them alone. We
should cast them on the Lord and take a rest.

Years ago it was a common thing for many for-
eigners to begin business in America as pack
peddlers. Some big businesses have had such
humble beginnings. One day in the deep South a
farmer with a good team and a new wagon was
returning home from the cotton gin. He entered a
long, hot dusty lane. Ahead, he saw a pack peddler
bent beneath his heavy load, trudging slowly. As
he pulled up to him, he stopped and said, "If you

23

would like to have a ride, climb in." The peddler climbed over the end gate, and the farmer continued his journey. After awhile the farmer looked back and the peddler was just sitting there crouched beneath his burden. Then the farmer said, "Wouldn't you like to take that pack off and take a rest?" The poor fellow replied, "Well, sir, I didn't know if you were willing to haul both me and my pack."

He did not know that it would make the load no heavier to lay the pack down and take a rest. It is easy for us to smile at this poor man. But what about us? Do we think it might be too burdensome for the Lord to carry both us and our cares? Poor souls! If the Lord is carrying us, He is already bearing our burdens. So it would make His load no heavier, if we would lay our pack of troubles down and take a needed rest.

Jesus says, "Come unto me, all ye that labor and are heavy laden, and I will give you rest" (Matthew 11:28).

Rest is a necessity in our being and in the nature of all things. The ground, vegetation, animals, and machinery need rest. Our body also demands rest. All human organs need rest. Because of this need, God has provided rest for us. He divided the time between day and night, and separated the year into planting, plowing, reaping, and respite. Even Christ had to withdraw from the multitudes to allow His body to rest.

◆

Nature, reason, and the Scriptures teach God's law of rest.

Our soul also needs rest. The toilsome journey of life amid vexations and heartaches demands rest for the soul. David had experienced this need. He said, "I was brought low, and he helped me. Return unto thy rest, O my soul; for the Lord hath dealt bountifully with thee. For thou hast delivered my soul from death, mine eyes from tears, and my feet from falling" (Psalms 116:6-8).

We need the rest; so let us confidently cast our burdens on the Lord.

• *We acquire courage from good friends who stand by us and support us.* The ancient Greeks symbolized true friendship by writing on the garment of a young man, "Summer and winter." When the storms of adversity beat the hardest, true friendships become the warmest and strongest. It would be hard for us to carry on without the aid of true friends. Our friends' letters, words, visits, and prayers mean so much.

The brotherhood of man demands that we respond to each other's joys and sorrows. The Bible says, "Rejoice with them that do rejoice, and weep with them that weep" (Romans 12:15). This is truly the Christian spirit. Jesus exemplified it at the tomb of Lazarus when He wept. So tears are sacred. Jesus wept because His great heart was touched. The sad tears from an aching heart and

◆

the sympathetic tears from a true friend become misty hues which form a beautiful rainbow reaching from one to the other.

The flowers live by the tears that fall
From the sad face of the skies,
And life would have no joys at all
Were there no watery eyes.

Love thou sorrow; grief shall bring
Its own excuse in after years—
The rainbow!— see how fair a thing
God hath built up from tears.

—SUTTON

The fact that we are all brothers in adversity inclines us to be friends whether we are acquainted or not. So in addition to our known friends we have many other friends we have not met. They are standing by just like the Samaritan who helped a stranger (Luke 10:29-37). When the occasion demands it, they will prove to be Good Samaritans and will come to our aid.

But in deede,
A friend is never known till a man have neede.

— HEYWOOD

• *We may think ourselves to victory over suffering.* Or we may think ourselves to defeat. Solomon

◆

said as a man "thinketh in his heart, so is he" (Proverbs 23:7). No one is ever stronger than his thoughts. Both cowards and heroes are the results of their thinking.

"When I live in a settled and steadfast assurance about the state of my soul, methinks I am as bold as a lion. I can laugh at all trouble; no affliction daunts me; but when I am eclipsed in my comforts, I am of so fearful a spirit that I could run into a mousehole."

— LATIMER TO RIDLEY.

"Stone walls do not a prison make, nor iron bars a cage." The world is filled with people who have become prisoners of their own thinking. Their own attitudes have imprisoned them. Prison bars of iron are hard and unyielding, but a thought is a stronger bar than one made of iron. One of the characters created by Charles Dickens was right when he said, "I wear the chain I forged in life." Indeed, we bind ourselves by the chains we forge. If we have become captives to our own thoughts of despair and defeat, we can never find freedom and relief until we change our thinking.

Self-pitiers are usually self-defeated persons. They usually imagine that they have the most difficulties, the hardest time, and the maximum of grief. Their longing for sympathy only deepens

◆

their gloom and defeat.

We need to say in the language of Paul, "I can do all things through Christ which strengtheneth me" (Philippians 4:13). There is power in saying, "I can." "I can't" has defeated many a person. Success comes in "cans"; failure comes in "can'ts."

We have strength — physical, moral, and mental — that we have never dreamed of. When the occasion calls for it, we can draw from that dormant strength through the power of victorious thinking. Whatever your problem is, say, "I can solve it." Whatever you sorrow is, say, "I can bear it." Whatever your suffering is, say, "I can endure it." Say, "I can; I can; I can." Say it again and again. You will be surprised at your invigoration and new outlook on life.

If you can force your heart and nerve and sinew
To serve your turn long after they are gone,
And so hold on when there is nothing in you
Except the will which says to them: "Hold on!"
Yours is the Earth and everything that's in it,
And — which is more — you'll be a Man,
my son!

— *If*, RUDYARD KIPLING

• *Gratitude for the blessings we have relieves the sting from the afflictions we must often suffer.* Gratitude to God not only honors Him, but blesses

◆

us. It is always refreshing to recall, "Every good gift and every perfect gift is from above, and cometh down from the Father" (James 1:17). May we never forget it.

No matter how heavy and low the clouds hang, the sun is shining somewhere. The Godward side of every cloud is always bright. Our afflictions may be numerous, but so are our blessings. Our sorrows may be heart-breaking, but our joys can be heart-healing. We have never seen circumstances so bad but what they could be worse. The author knows a young bedridden husband who has suffered physical agony for days and days which slowly pass; but he has smiles in his cheeks and a song in his heart because he is so grateful and happy to be alive. We have never known a person struck down so low but what he could find, if he would only look, many graces to raise him up.

Some people, however, destroy themselves through their own ingratitude. Ungratefulness robs us of one of the noblest qualities. Many people are miserable because they are unthankful. Any trait we cultivate will grow. As selfishness increases so does ingratitude. One feeds the other and both grow.

The ungrateful mind is always a discontented mind. It fails to recognize God's many blessings. The ungrateful person cannot enjoy the blessings he has for fretting over the blessings he does not

◆

have. The secret of gratitude is in making the most of what you have. The secret of contentment is in making the least of what you lack. A deep gratitude for what you have will take the fret out of what you lack.

If you have not health; if you no longer have father, mother, husband, wife, son, or daughter (death has taken them); if you have no financial or job security; then think upon all the blessings you do have and be grateful for them. It is then that you will find strength for your suffering. It is weakening to indulge in useless resentment over afflictions and adversities. The battle is half won by counting your blessings. Count them. You will be surprised.

CHAPTER FOUR

Compensations for Suffering

There are many blessings to be derived from sufferings, if we accept them analytically and gracefully. Otherwise, there is the danger of frustration and rebellion. The cynic is invariably a man whose hopes have been thwarted. It is our reactions to our troubles that either help or harm us. The same sun that melts the tallow hardens the clay. The same experience suffered by two persons may be the means of softening one and hardening the other.

> *Life is a mirror; if you frown at it, it frowns back; if you smile, it returns the greeting.*
> — THACKERAY

If we are made of the right stuff, distress can help us to discover the pearls of life.

◆

The burden of suffering seems a tombstone hung about our necks, while in reality it is only the weight which is necessary to keep down the diver while he is hunting for pearls.

— RICHTER.

• *Through sickness people may become better acquainted with themselves.* Modern life is lived at high speed. There is so much hurry and rush over things that are relatively unimportant. Life's competition has never before been so keen and strenuous. Consequently, many of life's toilers are pushing themselves to the breaking point — nervous indigestion, stomach ulcers, tattered nerves, and sleepless nights. The cares of the world are written all over their faces. Little time for prayer, Bible reading, and deep meditation which feeds the soul! The mad rush of a chaotic civilization has estranged them from their deeper self. They have been strangers to themselves.

Then sickness comes. The wheels of a busy routine are slowed down. This enforced idleness compels them to think, think, and think. Through thinking they become acquainted with themselves all over again. They come to know the real meaning of life. They learn their true self and what their real needs are — that they have longings for peace of heart which can never be satisfied with the material things of life. From their own feelings, they learn how wrong the rich man of the Bible and

◆

a million others have been who said, "Soul, thou hast much goods laid up for many years; take thine ease, eat, drink, and be merry" (Luke 12:19). They learn there is a part of man that cannot live on the things you stack in barns and banks. Their sense of proportion comes back to them.

They have learned the hard way! But they have learned! So if a fevered and restless brow has helped to cool and calm a fevered and restless soul, then the suffering has not been in vain. If sickness has led one to know himself, then it has truly had its compensation.

Know thyself!

• *Distress may help us to better know the Lord.* Through our veil of tears, we see in a new light Him who was "despised and rejected of men; a man of sorrows, and acquainted with grief" (Isaiah 53:3). We become better acquainted with Christ when we experience His teaching, love, and sympathy in times of suffering and sorrow. In suffering Jesus becomes a necessity to us — not just a half-hearted luxury. We come to know Him better, because we need Him more. Through pain we feel a more appreciative touch of His hand. Through the agony of our afflictions we hear a new tenderness in His voice. Through the recognition of our own helplessness we feel a new strength in His strong arms about us.

A blind man once said, "I never did see until I became blind." Not until this affliction came upon him was he able to get his eyes of discernment

◆

open. Not until he became blind to one world was he able to see another. When his material eyes were closed, his spiritual eyes were opened. Then for the first time he was able to see the invisible.

Paul said, "While we look not at the things which are seen, but at the things which are not seen; for the things which are seen are temporal; but the things which are not seen are eternal" (II Corinthians 4:18).

Suffering and sorrow lend a new appreciation to Paul's words. They enable us to have a better sense of values.

It was Moses' ability to see the unseen that inspired him to choose wisely and that sustained him in his afflictions. The Bible says, "For he endured, as seeing him who is invisible" (Hebrews 11:27).

Suffering has the power to teach us our inadequacy. It shows us that we have trusted in our weak humanity too long. It proves to us that we need help we cannot muster and power that we cannot generate. Our distress may encourage us to trust in the Lord, for it shows the folly of trusting in self. If it has that effect, then the sufferer has been rewarded.

Trust in the Lord with all thine heart; and lean not unto thine own understanding.

PROVERBS 3:5

◆

• *Sickness may be the means of cultivating friendships.* Kind and loving friends come to our assistance and help us carry our burdens. Never before did a kind word, a warm handshake, and sympathetic prayer mean so much. Friendships take on a greater value.

These words have so often come from the lips of the sick, "I never knew I had so many friends." Well, they had been standing by all the time. Maybe the sick person had allowed those friendships to get in bad repair — not intentionally but through neglect. Now he vows that when he gets well he is going to be a better friend, that he is going to visit the sick more, and that he is going to do more to help others. Good vows! Those who have been awakened to make them should keep them.

If illness leads us to repair friendships, then this unhappy experience has had another reward.

A man that hath friends must show himself friendly.

PROVERBS 18:24

• *Suffering may mellow our hearts and lend a new warmth to our services.* We cannot fully understand the other person's problems until we have experienced similar ones. We shall never know how heavy another's burdens are until those weights have rested on our own shoulders. Distress may add tenderness to our hearts and nobility to our lives. It can bring us closer together. And appreciation and sympathy are impossible at arm's length.

The Bible commands us, "Rejoice with them that do rejoice, and weep with them that weep" (Romans 12:15).

This is truly the Christian spirit and one of the world's greatest needs. In a cold and heartless world the agonizing hearts of many are crying out for sympathy and understanding. Our own experiences of pain, disappointment, and sorrow better qualify us to answer those calls.

Years ago a widowed mother lost her only child. To her, the thought of God became irony and the idea of life became mockery. She needed sympathetic understanding. She was icily told as she wept over her child, "You ought to say, 'Thy will be done'." Like a tearing tigress, she turned on her would-be-consoler and said, "Could you?"

The advice was unquestionably good, but there was no compassion in it. It was like water flowing from a mountain of ice. The water is pure, but it is cold.

Later another went to her and said, "Do not blame yourself if you feel rebellious. God knows your loss and He will not blame you for your grief." She gladly turned to that man and listened intently. Why? Because, he, like Jesus, was a "man of sorrows and acquainted with grief." His sympathetic

◆

words fell affectionately upon responsive ears that would have been closed by the coldness of those without hearts.

It is a law as old as humanity that it takes a heart to touch a heart. Hence, a full head can never take the place of an empty heart. A man with a big heart is a big man.

CHAPTER FIVE

"Be of Good Cheer"

$\mathcal{A}$s a small boy was eating his dinner, the sparkling, golden rays of the setting sun fell upon his spoon. He put the spoon to his mouth and playfully exclaimed in his childish make-believe, "Mamma, I have swallowed a spoonful of sunshine." How excellent it would be if many of us grown-ups could swallow a few spoonfuls of sunshine. It would do some of us more good than medicine. The wise man Solomon had this in mind when he said, "A merry heart doeth good like a medicine: but a broken spirit drieth the bones" (Proverbs 17:22). Cheerfulness contributes to sanity and good health. It doubles the value of food and sleep, lightens the burden of every care, and gives the heart courage to face every problem.

There is dismay sometimes for which we are not responsible. Circumstances place us amid

conditions which are most disheartening. Some-times this cannot be avoided. But the vast majority of gloomy people simply "achieve" dismay. They have made themselves wretched; they have brought it upon themselves; and they alone are to blame for being miserable.

It is natural that unhappy people ask the cause of this dismay. David did. He sought an explanation of his depression by asking, "Why are thou cast down, O my soul? And why art thou disquieted within me?" (Psalms 42:5). Why? Yes, why are we sorrowful?

• *One thing that causes low spirits is sin.* Remorse gnaws at the heart. Conscience can make wretches of us all. And there is no satisfying relief until we experience the healing cure of forgiveness. When forgiven, then we should put it behind us. There was enough sin in the apostle Paul's past to forever make him miserable — that is, if he had brooded over it. But by the grace of God he received forgiveness, and he put it behind him, forgot it, and reached forth to the things before him (Philippians 3:13,14). This is the only happy way to live. One great reason for rejoicing is forgiveness.

• *Another everyday cause of dismay with many people is conceit.* In this case, gloom is the product of an exaggerated egotism.

A gentleman once told of entering a room of mirrors, and he saw himself reflected twelve or fifteen times. The room was filled with himself. No

◆

one else was in the room. Of course, he was pleased with such agreeable company.

Most people enjoy being the "whole show." But if someone even hints that they are not as brilliant or important as they think they are, they become most miserable. Man's egotism causes him to demand special attention from his friends. They have to dust off the chair for him. But it is not long until that is not enough. Then they have to go up and dust off the clouds for him, because that is where his head is. If they refuse, then he feels that he is not appreciated, and frets and snarls at everything and everybody.

The conceit of many has robbed them of much sunshine. Their state is aptly described by what Canovas said of Castello, the Spanish politician. He said that Castello was so anxious for notice and high position that he could not enjoy a wedding, because, not being the bridegroom, he could not receive most attention; and that he could not appreciate a funeral, because he was not the corpse about whom the most of the people were thinking.

God's remedy for this trouble is found in the Bible: "For I say, through the grace given unto me, to every man that is among you, not to think of himself more highly than he ought to think" (Romans 12:3).

• *Another cause of mental depression is an exaggerated inferiority complex.* We say "exaggerated," because perhaps every person has an inferiority complex. The difference is that some

exaggerate it. Yes, some may appear to have a superiority complex and take on the brass and bluster of a superman, but perhaps beneath the surface there is that deep and common feeling of inferiority. But inferiority can be adjusted to the honor and achievement of man.

Admittedly, there are diversities of gifts. "All members have not the same office" (Romans 12:4,5). Thus we may need to change goals in life. If we cannot be an Abraham Lincoln or a Babe Ruth, we can be a useful and honored minister, physician, carpenter, farmer, nurse, seamstress, or homemaker. Man is so constituted that he desires admiration and honor from others, and this may be obtained by doing a job well. A goal should be attainable; otherwise, it only increases a feeling of inferiority and frustration.

If we have either a real or fancied deficiency let us recognize it and then find the way out. It is in the good interest of humanity that different people have different talents and different degrees of ability (Matthew 25:14-30). If we are only one talent people, we must accept it. We can come to grips with our deficiency and make it pay off. It can be a tremendous motivating power in life, if we are prepared to put the necessary drive behind it.

Angelo Siciliano, better known as Charles Atlas, is a most encouraging example. At sixteen he was a ninety-seven pound runt, and a common victim of the bullies' rough stuff. But while visiting in the Brooklyn Museum he got a vision of

◆

strength. He saw the statues of Apollo and Hercules. He was told that young Greek athletes had served as models for the statues. That very day he began taking exercises according to instructions he found in a newspaper. Sarcasm and ridicule did not daunt him. He did not give up. Later he invented his own exercises. He became the mighty Atlas and "the world's most perfectly developed man." Why was he able to achieve this? Because his feeling of inferiority motivated him to great effort.

It is a law of nature that ability and talent can increase. The weakness of one arm may lead to the strength of the other. Blindness has its compensation in the development of keener senses of touch and hearing. One weak lung is offset by the increased strength of the other. What is true of us physically can also be true of us emotionally.

The possibilities of superiority through compensation for inferiority is illustrated in some of the best known lives in history. The biographies of Aristotle, Wagner, Stevenson, Pope, Bacon, Parkman, and Keats indicate that their lives were shaped by their disabilities. Alexander and Napoleon found military greatness in their struggle to seek compensation for smallness of stature. Even the unusual ugliness of Socrates and Voltaire spurred them to develop their history-making abilities.

Man alone has the feeling of inferiority, and man alone attempts to compensate for it. It can be the spark in your life to ignite a power that you did not know you had.

• *Another reason for gloom with many people is the folly of borrowing trouble.* "It is ills that never happened that have mostly made men miserable," says Tupper. Never borrow trouble. The calamity you dread may never come. If it should come, it is folly to pay interest on it in advance. If it does come tomorrow, you will be better able to meet it by reserving today's strength.

Many people are miserable because they try to cross all their bridges before they get to them. To them life seems unbearable, because they view it in the lump. They remind us of a story in one of McGuffey's old readers about a clock which suddenly stopped. From the dialogue in the story we learn that the clock became discouraged after having counted the number of times it would have to tick in one year — 31,560,000 times — just too many ticks for any old clock. However, when it was explained to the clock that it would have to tick only one tick at a time, it regained its morale and began keeping time again. Now, there is a lesson for us. All that is expected of us is to do right now and meet present problems and duties. No one has the strength to carry the weight of all that might happen in the future.

Jesus taught us this lesson: "Sufficient unto the day is the evil thereof" (Matthew 6:34) This does not encourage laziness or irresponsibility. Instead, it teaches us to live life a day at a time. After

◆

all, this is the only way it can be lived. Yesterday cannot be lived for it is gone. Tomorrow cannot be lived for it has not come. All that we have is today. And the best preparation we can make for the future is to take care of our duties today. Hold your imagination in check. This makes life cheerful.

• *Another thing that disquiets the souls of some is the harboring of malice.* There can be no inward peace when one is filled with hatred. We are smart if we free ourselves of that which would warp our personality and destroy us. Some return evil for evil at the dear price of destroying themselves. They get even by pulling themselves down to the level of their enemies.

It is no marvel that God has said, "Recompense to no man evil for evil . . . Vengeance is mine; I will repay, saith the Lord" (Romans 12:17-19). This is for our welfare. And happy is the one who abides by it.

If you have been pondering a wrong you have suffered, forget it. No one has been mistreated and wronged more than Joseph — and that by his own family. His brothers, motivated by envy, sold him into slavery. But he did not waste his life plotting and scheming to get vengeance. He was not willing for hatred to make him a greater slave. He forgot it. When his firstborn son came, he named him "Manasseh," for he said that God had made him forget (Genesis 41:51).

A man once went to President Lincoln and stated that he had been abused by a congressman

◆

and wanted his advice. Lincoln said, "Write out the account and bring it to me." This was done and the President read the paper. Lincoln then said, "That is good; now take it home — keep it till tomorrow, read it, then burn it."

We are in the pursuit of happiness if we learn to forget the wrongs we suffer.

CHAPTER SIX

Motives to Cheerfulness

*N*o matter what happens, keep up your courage. Be brave. Bravery leads to victory, but cowardice leads to defeat. Shakespeare profoundly expressed it in these words:

> *Cowards die many times before their death,*
> *The valiant never taste of death but once.*

Cowards die a thousand times before death really comes. Through their own temperament they assign themselves to the narrow and harassing confines of a living death. This kind of dying — death of faith, death of hope, death of cheer, death of personality — is worse than death of body.

Life is sacred and time is precious, too precious to waste any of it by making ourselves a kind of

◆

living corpse which does little more than breathe and stare. So let us live while we live, for death will come soon enough.

There are so many things to stimulate us to cheerfulness; for instance:

• *One motive to cheerfulness is that others have* troubles as well as we — not that we rejoice in others' adversities, but it does help us to understand that we are no different from others. A suffering world pictures to us the realities of life. It teaches us that life must be lived in the world of reality rather than spent in sheltered dream castles. Trouble is one thing to which all of us are heir. Your neighbor may not have your troubles, but he has his own which may be worse than yours. Trouble is visited alike on the rich and the poor, the high and the lowly — there is no exception.

A king, riding in his splendid and costly chariot, passed a stone cutter by the side of the road. As the man of toil looked up he said to himself, "Oh, if I could be like that man — no work, no problems, no worries." Just at that moment the king looked down and said to himself, "Oh, if I could have been born like that man — no problems, no cares; work is so much sweeter than worry." It is true that the king had no problem in paying his grocery bill and his house rent, but had the worries of forty million people and the problem of retaining his crown.

Others have their burdens, and they bear them. So can you. No burden is too heavy to bear. The

trouble is that we often think ourselves too weak to carry it. An elderly lady who had been confined to her sick bed for many months pointed to a bird outside the window and said, "I love that robin because he sings in the rain."

When we learn to sing in the rain we have made real progress in the development of personality. So bear your troubles bravely and with a hopeful heart. If you wait until you have no troubles to be cheerful, then your days will never be blessed with cheer. Instead, your life will be a continuous nightmare of despondency, for there will be no dawning of troubleless days in this life. Remember — this earth is not heaven.

• *Another incentive producing cheerfulness is that it honors Christianity.* A gloomy, bitter, pessimistic person is not a good advertisement for Christianity. If Christianity has done that to him, then be not surprised that the world will not want it. But we hasten to say that Christianity has never produced despair and sourness in any life. A perverted notion of Christianity has produced it — but not true Christianity.

Years ago a little girl looked out the window and saw a mule grazing in the pasture nearby. She said, "Grandpa, is that old mule a Christian too?" "Oh! No! Why do you say that?" was the answer. The little girl thought-provokingly replied: "Well, I thought maybe he was, because his face is so long."

◈

She was being impressed with a form of mis-interpreted Christianity — perverted teachings, because true Christianity is a religion of cheer. Jesus said, "Be of good cheer." The person who sincerely embraces Christ's teaching and follows it is possessed with a power which produces cheerfulness. "And he went on his way rejoicing," is said of the man who accepted the faith of Christianity, being baptized by Philip (Acts 8:39).

The sad, gloomy, dejected person is no shining light for Christianity. Contrariwise, he advertises to the world that his religion — if he follows any — is too weak to sustain him in adverse circumstances. On the other hand, Christianity will support us — that is, if we support it.

• *Another inducement to a sunny disposition is that we may not be as bad off as we think.* You may have magnified your troubles. You may have let your imagination run wild. Your true condition may be much better than you have supposed. So cheer up. Get your mind off your troubles. Think on the bright things in life. Be grateful for the good things you have. Your worrying over one thing you lack may have caused you to forget so many things you have. There is a lesson for us in the proverb: "I complained because I had no shoes until I saw a man who had no feet."

• *Another stimulant to high spirits is the indisputable fact that it pays.* Some virtues may delay their day of compensation, but cheerfulness pays

now. Its dividends are inestimable. Hanway said, "Good-nature is the beauty of the mind, and, like personal beauty, wins almost without anything else, — sometimes, indeed, in spite of positive deficiencies."

Cheerfulness pays by prolonging life. Doctors prescribe merriment for their patients. Solomon said, "A merry heart doeth good like a medicine: but a broken spirit drieth the bones" (Proverbs 17:22). Science shows that our moods affect our health.

A bright outlook pays in that it minimizes our troubles. A sick man once said, "I have asthma, gout, and six other maladies, but otherwise I am very well." Through his own outlook he lessened his burdens.

A sunny spirit will also pay us in friends. The cheerful person has a magnetism that pulls us to him. But the gloomy person repels us.

Laugh and the world laughs with you;
Weep and you weep alone.
For that sad old earth must borrow its mirth,
But has trouble enough of its own.

—*Solitude,* ELLA WHEELER WILCOX

• *The promise that God will not leave us, nor forsake us is another one of the many motives*

◆

prompting good cheer. God has said to His people, "I will never leave thee, nor forsake thee" (Hebrews 13:5). So take courage and be brave. When our human weaknesses seem so inadequate for life's problems and our heart is struck with fear, let us repeat this promise again and again.

A young husband and father lost in death his faithful companion and the sweet mother of his little girl. After the funeral service had been concluded, they tearfully left that hallowed soil of the silent city of the dead to plod their way homeward once again. The sun was a ball of fire in the west. Night with its fears and depressing effects was rapidly falling. He tried to eat even though he had no appetite. He read her a little story in spite of the fact that his heart was breaking within him. He had to be brave for her sake. Bedtime came and he tucked his little daughter in her bed as best weary and clumsy hands could. The lights were turned out.

There were only a few moments of silence and she said, "Daddy, are you still there? It is so dark and I am so afraid." The father replied, "Yes, honey, I am still here." Then her little anxious heart gave expression to this question, "Daddy, will you be with me all during the night?" He was quick to explain that he would and that when morning came he would still be there. Then in her effort to be brave and cheerful she replied, "Daddy, if you are going to be with me all night, then I'll hush crying

and go to sleep." In a little while she was asleep.

Then the father knelt down beside his bed and prayed, "Oh, God, it is so dark and I am so afraid, but if you will be with me all during the night, I, too, shall hush crying and go to sleep."

This man's bitter and trying experience shows to some extent the significance of God's promise to be with us. What a stimulant to keep up the fight! What a powerful impulse to cheerfulness. Assurance greater than man! For this is divine assurance. And we truly need it. May we so live that God can walk by our side. He will not forsake us. Let us be sure that we do not forsake Him.

• *Hope is another powerful impulse to cheerfulness.* Hope and gladness go together. Solomon said, "The hope of the righteous shall be gladness" (Proverbs 10:28).

Hope is the quality which makes life worthwhile. It fills our untoward days with happy anticipations. Civilization rests on hope. The farmer plows in hope. Last year the insects destroyed his crops. The year before the floods washed them away. And the year before that the drought stunted their growth. But he plows and plants in hope. He tells himself that it will be better this year. Every business is founded on hope. The merchant rents a building, buys stock, and opens the doors for business on hope. If all hope were crushed, all humanity would die. It is essential to life.

Hope gives us strength to "bear those ills we

◆

have," because we look forward to a better day. A dear lady who had been confined to her bed and forced to lie on one side for several days said, "Oh! I am so happy. The doctor said that if no complications arise and that if I continue to improve, I can be turned over on my other side next week." How wonderful! She could have fretted and made herself miserable by thinking about her present discomforts. Instead, she hoped for a brighter day and in hope she found steadfastness and cheer. Her mood was controlled by her outlook on life. That is true of all of us. Both cheer and despondency are not dependent upon outside circumstances. They are the result of inside jobs. So if we can control the problems within us, then we shall have no real trouble in controlling the problems that are without.

No matter what our burden is, hope for something better, and we will find it. First, we will find that our present distress is nothing like as trying as we had thought. The person with hope never knows when he is licked, and for that reason he isn't. He just keeps on fighting. He knows that no road is so long but that it finally passes. He finds cheerfulness in hope, because they go together.

'Tis always morning somewhere, and above
The awakening continents, from shore to
*   shore,*
Somewhere the birds are singing evermore.

◆

• *Another one of the many motives prompting a sunshiny spirit is the thought of eternal salvation.* Every suffering, every disappointment, and every sorrow seems so trivial and insignificant in comparison with the thought of going home to heaven. Hence, an apostle wrote, "For our light affliction, which is but for a moment, worketh for us a far more exceeding and eternal weight of glory; while we look not at the things which are seen, but at the things which are not seen: for the things which are seen are temporal; but the things which are not seen are eternal" (II Corinthians 4:17,18). These afflictions are but for a moment, comparatively speaking. By keeping our eyes on heaven we get them off our adversities. This is why they seem but light afflictions for only a moment. Despite the trials of the past and the toils and disappointments of the present, the anticipations of going home put a sparkle in our eyes, a smile in our cheeks, and a song on our lips. This earth is not our home. Here we are just pilgrims passing through a barren land. The thought of going home is cheering.

Even a horse travels better when his head is toward home. His day's work in the field may have been hard and the journey home is long. But the heavy work of the day and the long road home seem as nothing when once his head is pointed in that direction. His whole attitude changes; his head is lifted; his eyes and ears are turned forward; and

he quickens his pace.

Likewise, how cheering to the suffering heart of a Christian is the thought of going home. He counts not the battles he has fought with sin and Satan. He no longer sees the scars he suffered in the fight. He has forgotten the reproaches and persecutions of sinners. He thinks not upon the heartwounds that bled him by the way. Nothing can deter him. He is going home! And all is well!

CHAPTER SEVEN

Inner Peace

We are living in a complex age. Modern civilization is crowded with problems. But the greatest problem is man himself. All other problems are comparatively insignificant. The world's greatest fear is not the bomb, but the man who handles it. The power of atoms handled by a saint constitutes less threat to civilization than a small pistol handled by a criminal. Therefore, if we would help the world, we must help man; and if we would save the world, we must save man.

• *Our greatest need in this warring world is not world peace but inner peace.* Peace of soul comes first. Man struggles with man because first of all the struggle rages within himself. Cain had trouble with his brother Abel and slew him (Genesis 4:1-8), because Cain first of all had

trouble with himself — the trouble of envy and hatred. This first murderer's own inner conflict alienated him from his brother. Frustrated souls almost without an exception blame everybody but themselves for their troubles. They cannot have peace with others because they are not at peace with themselves. The battle in the field is the outgrowth of the battle in the heart.

The very nature of sin is such that it intensifies the sinner's opposition to the righteous. This happened to Cain. The cause of his frustration was within himself. The passing of the centuries has not changed man. The problems of the past will always be the problems of the present and of the future. We have new people, but the same old problems — external conflicts which are born of the frustration within our hearts.

What can be done to take us off the treadmill of fears, nerves, and frustrations? How can we cure the frightening anxieties and find peace of soul? First, we must learn the cause of frustration. If we cure the cause, the effect will take care of itself. Since we are no different from the people of the Bible, then we can go to the Bible and find both the cause and its cure.

• *The case of the Prodigal Son is enlightening* (Luke 15). He became alienated from himself, and this led him to withdraw from others and from God. His inner conflict had its beginning in his departing from himself. Not having any great objective in life,

he heard the call of many voices. And he began to answer them, but none would satisfy. His life became locked in a prison of self, and this shut him off from others and from God. Estrangement from others and God are sure to result when we live only for ourselves and for this world. He asked for his part of the estate. It was given to him. He left his father and family, friends and country. But neither life nor money was used for good. He wasted his days and his money in riotous living. It brought him low, to starvation, disgrace, and to a friendless state. In his blind and reckless search for inner peace he merely drove himself farther from it. Life became cruel to him because he was cruel to it.

After reaching the hog-pen level in life, "he came to himself." This is the key that unlocked the prison of his own making. He came back to his better self. He thought of home, his early training, helpful service to others, honest toil, clean relationships, and the days when his conscience was clear. Those were the good days. The only wise thing was to travel the hard road back to his former state. To refuse would have only aggravated his troubles. He had to go back or his condition would have worsened. So his way was clear. He said, "I will arise and go to my Father, and will say unto him, Father, I have sinned against heaven, and before thee, and am no more worthy to be called thy son: make me as one of thy hired servants."

The Prodigal's getting away from his better self

had its roots in his getting away from God. We were created in the spiritual image of God. We are spirit as well as flesh. Hence, living solely for the flesh will never satisfy our deeper longings. Some, not willing to return to the Father as did the Prodigal Son, have sought escape from their god-lessness in violent hatred of God and severe perse-cution of religion. This, however, has never brought them peace — just more trouble.

Let us note what is implied in the young man's going back home. He came to himself — rational thinking. He went back to man from whom he had departed — sociable thinking. He went back to humility — claimed nothing big, no veneered righ-teousness, no complex. He went back to the fields of toil — honest labor. He went back to a busy and fruitful life — idleness was no fun. He went back to face the realities of life. He went back to God, for the father in the parable represents God. He went back to his true self.

What did he leave? He left egotism — his "ego" was not practical, just a false front that anyone could see through. He left idleness — it had only increased his miseries. He left a dream world — because life is real. He left a false view of living — he learned that to eat, drink, and be merry are not the true ends of living. He left behind his material conception of happiness — he acquired the much-needed lesson that happiness comes from being neither rich nor poor, for he had vainly tried both.

◆

He left selfishness — from his grim experiences, he learned that the world did not revolve around himself. He left a life of sin — it had not satisfied. Summed up, he left behind a perverted self.

He came to himself. He went back home, and he found peace.

• *If we find peace, we must find it within ourselves.* The Prodigal Son found it right where he had left it — within himself. Every one who loses peace, does so through his own thinking. To regain peace, we must change our thinking and come to ourselves. This enables us to come back to God and to man. The thing the Prodigal wanted most was at first too close for him to see it. Oftentimes there is gold at our feet that we cannot see, because we look beyond it.

We knew a man who literally did this. He spent a lifetime looking for literal gold. With pick in hand, he diligently sought the magic ore in the hills, breaks and streams in the Red River country. Finally he stumbled on what he thought to be the precious metal. His find was kept very secret. But the assayer said, "It is not gold; it is a metal called fool's gold." He first tried not to believe it, but there was no alternative. Facts are facts. He finally died a broken, disappointed, poverty-stricken old man. The irony of it is that shortly after he died, a well was drilled on his little farm, and a new kind of gold — oil, flowing black gold — was found in abundant quantities. Gold was there at his feet, but

◆

he never found it because he never thought of looking for it at home.

While this was literally true of this one man, it is figuratively and spiritually true of millions of others. They seek this inner peace in every place except their inner self. The paradoxical thing is that it is there in their own heart where they left it and can be found only by returning to it. Any outward peace they have found is merely superficial.

• *The world is filled with lessons which teach us that peace does not depend upon outside circumstances.* This is seen in the works of two painters. Each painted a picture to portray his conception of true peace. The first chose for his painting a still, peaceful, lone lake high up in the mountains. The second painted on his canvas a rushing, roaring waterfall, with an uncertain and fragile tree bending over the white foam. A robin sat on its nest at the fork of the branch.

The first was only stillness. The second was true peace — peace unrelated to outside circumstances. The little bird knew no anxiety. The twig on which he rested seemed unsafe to us. But there as he tossed and swayed in the wind, he joyously sang. He was indifferent to the water's spray and the twig's bend. For he had wings folded at his side. If he fell, he simply fell on his power to be lifted heavenward; for the sky was his home. This was peace which came from within.

◆

Be like the bird, who
Halting in his flight
On limb too slight
Feels it give way beneath him,
Yet sings
Knowing he hath wings.

— VICTOR HUGO

The life of Jesus was like that second painting. He was superior to all storms and trials because He had wings. No other man has had such serenity of soul, and no other man has had such a hectic stay in a restless world. Outwardly, Christ's life was filled with conflicts. Inwardly, there was peace as calm as a sea of glass. And even when His enemies were hounding Him for His life, He turned to troubled men, and as a last legacy offered them peace. He said, "Peace I leave with you, my peace I give unto you" (John 14:27).

CHAPTER EIGHT

Suggestions for Inner Peace

The world is filled with people who pace themselves like an imprisoned lion within his cage. They are seeking release from an unknown something, which is actually themselves. They imprisoned themselves through their own thoughts, attitudes, and ways of living.

Now they seek escape. They want something more satisfying than food and freedom, strength and security. They want a food different from that the world lives on — they want food which feeds the soul. They long for a freedom that civilization as a whole does not know — freedom of mind. They want a new kind of strength and security, yet it is old — the strength and security which comes from within. They want to be something. They want something to live with, and something to live for. They want peace!

Their cries for help are heard the world over. A thousand answers come back. But only a few offer anything worthwhile. Not finding the constructive answer, they often enslave themselves all the more to drink, gambling, lust, strife, hate, envy, jealousy, suspicion, and bitterness. They resent the world and complain about it. But if they will become different, they will find the world different. Thus we offer these suggestions from God's Book on better living:

• *Make up your mind to be happy.* What you decide will largely influence your state. For as a man "thinketh in his heart, so is he" (Proverbs 23:7). One can think himself into being miserable. A man once said, "When I feel good, I always feel bad; because I know that I am going to feel worse later." His thinking did this to him. The pessimist is always a creature of his own thinking.

• *Begin to cultivate peace within yourself now.* It is not a luxury to be denied for sixty years because you are unable to afford it now. Habits grow, and one who says "tomorrow" will soon make tomorrow the rule of life. He who waits until tomorrow yields to a mischievous illusion. There is no such day as tomorrow; it is only a mirage, a fool's paradise. Yesterday is buried, tomorrow is unborn; therefore, today holds life and death, peace and conflict in its living hands. One of the great words in the Bible is "today."

• *Learn that inner peace is mental rather than geographical.* "Oh! that I were somewhere else," is

◆

the attitude of the malcontents. If they live in the country, they spend years trying to get to the city; if they get to the city, then they spend the rest of their lives trying to save enough to get back to the country. Contentment does not depend upon where you are, but rather upon what you are. This is why a man of the Bible who had faced strong opposition much of his life could say, "I have learned, in whatsoever state I am, therewith to be content" (Philippians 4:11).

Fixed to no spot is happiness sincere
'Tis nowhere to be found, or everywhere;
'Tis never to be bought, but always free.

—POPE

• *Be yourself.* God made us different. No two people are exactly alike. Each must be himself to be happy. Certainly this does not bar self-improvement; but as one improves, he does it as himself. If you are yourself, then you will not have to worry about false pretenses. Contentment is derived from doing things your own way. Mass imitation or conformity is having a powerful impact on man's emotional well-being. It is developing within him hesitancy, tenseness, and insecurity. He is never sure of himself until he learns the wishes of others, to do right and trust in God. Then we can boldly say, "The Lord is my helper, and I will not fear what man shall do unto me" (Hebrews 13:6).

◆

• *Accept yourself as you are.* An acceptance of self is essential to contentment. We must accept the fact that different people have different talents and different degrees of ability (Matthew 25:14-30). We must reconcile ourselves to our own limitations.

Self-acceptance means that we shall not indulge in useless worry over what nature did not give us. Some things cannot be helped. For instance, Jesus said, "Which of you by taking thought can add one cubit unto his stature?" Worrying about our height will make us neither taller nor shorter. We are on the road to happiness if we accept ourselves as we are, even though we have severe handicaps. A lady once said that the happiest day of her life was the day she accepted her homeliness.

In accepting self we should turn our obstacles into steppingstones. Fanny J. Crosby, the famous song writer, became blind at six weeks of age. In later years she testified: "I am the happiest soul living. If I had not been deprived of my sight, I would never have received so good an education, nor have been able to do good to so many people." This was so much better than despair which could have driven her to the streets to beg. Whatever our handicap is, accept it; conquer it; turn it into a victory. May we accept ourselves as we are and work from there.

• *Make the least of what you lack.* We do not need very much and do not need that little very long. A man of good circumstances once said, "I

◆

look at what I lack and count myself unhappy. Others look at what I have and count me happy." We have great difficulty in defining "enough." After all, real riches are in the mind — in the mind's attitude. Contentment consists not in multiplying our wealth, but in decreasing our wants.

True happiness is to no place confined;
But still is found in a contented mind.

• *Make the most of what you have.* Peace of mind comes from using what we possess. The five-talent man could say, "Lord, thou deliverest unto me five talents: behold, I have gained beside them five talents more" (Matthew 25:20). This accomplishment was a matter of great satisfaction to him. Neither riches nor poverty has the inherent power to make any mortal happy. Instead, happiness comes from making the most of what we have, whether little or much. While it is evident that wealth is a very convenient thing, it is also admitted that the poor man who enjoys his little is much richer than the wealthy man who gets no joy from his plenty. So the only standard by which we can conclude when we are really rich is peace of mind.

• *So live that your conscience will approve.* Many frustrated lives have their roots in a condemning conscience. Since man must live with himself, then he ought to keep himself fit to live with. "Beloved, if our heart condemn us not, then

◆

have we confidence toward God" (I John 3:21).

• *Be unselfish.* Through selfishness we destroy ourselves. It reminds us of the two goats which met on a narrow bridge high over a river. Neither would give way to the other. The result: selfishness destroyed them both. Selfishness destroys character, shrinks the soul, and makes us miserable. The one who seeks joy for self only, loses it. On the other hand, he who drives away the clouds for others will make some sunshine for himself. "Look not every man on his own things, but every man also on the things of others" (Philippians 2:4) is the happiest way to live.

• *Keep busy in profitable works.* Idleness is an enemy of contentment. The most miserable people in the world are those who have nothing to do but to have a good time. Our take-it-easy complex has led to more licentious living, wickedness, and crime. A nation that had a philosophy of work did not have so much restlessness and discontent; neither was it plagued with so many ulcers and nervous breakdowns; nor were there so many skid rows and jails. God's law of work is essential to our happiness (II Thessalonians 3:11,12).

Make use of time, let not advantage slip;
Beauty within itself should not be wasted;
Fair flowers, that are not gath'rd in their prime
Rot and consume themselves in little time.
— SHAKESPEARE

◆

• *Let the past lie behind you.* "Forgetting the things which are behind" is a necessary principle of happy living (Philippians 3:13). One of the greatest of all arts is the art of forgetting. If we have made mistakes, derive what wisdom we can from them and forget them. If we have sinned, comply with God's law of pardon so that we may receive forgiveness. Then forget it. When God forgives sin He remembers it no more. We should forget it too! Almost every life has its own closet of skeletons. We should not try to resurrect them. They belong to the never-changing past. What counts is what we do with today.

> *Life, like war, is a series of mistakes; and he is not the best Christian nor the best general who makes the fewest false steps. He is the best who wins the most splendid victories by the retrieval of mistakes.*
>
> — F.W. ROBERTSON

• *Maintain a noble relationship with God.* This sums it up, for it is our whole duty (Ecclesiastes 12:13). This is the one duty out of which all other duties grow. He who keeps it keeps himself and in so doing finds inner peace. But "the way of the transgressor is hard." Sin is the most deceitful master with which we must deal. It offers joy but gives sorrow; holds out peace but gives frustration.

◆

Fools make a mock at sin, will not believe
It carries such a dagger in its sleeve.
"How can it be," say they, "that such a thing,
So full of sweetness, e'er should have a sting?"
They know not that it is the very spell
Of sin to make men laugh themselves to hell.

From the foregoing principles, it is easy to see that contentment is a by-product. Thus happiness sought for happiness' sake is never found. Rather, happiness has a way of fleeing from those who directly seek it. It must be obtained indirectly or not at all. Just do your duty in life, and happiness will come.

"Be of Good Courage"

$\mathcal{T}$his was God's message to Joshua. Heavy responsibilities weighed upon Joshua, enough to frighten any man. The job cut out for him demanded heroism. He needed courage. So God spoke these assuring words: "Be strong and of good courage; be not afraid, neither be thou dismayed: for the Lord thy God is with thee whithersoever thou goest" (Joshua 1:9).

• *Courage is one of our direst needs,* because fear is one of our deadliest foes. Courage is a basic trait of a strong character. Physical courage enables a person to triumph over the fear of risking life for a person or cause. Moral courage gives us power to stand against society's criticism, ridicule, and persecution. Another type of courage is just plain old everyday courage which leads us to be brave amid all the wear and strain, friction and opposition of

◆

life. He who fights well his own battle of life is no less a hero than the person who fights in national armies. Heroism is where you find it, and not necessarily behind a gun. The daily circumstances of some people demand a type of courage unexcelled. They have brave hearts or they would give up the fight. The discouraged man simply lacks courage; and he becomes anxious and fearful. This disqualifies him for his best work.

• *Fear is a paralyzing thing.* We may be struck by many storms which do not wreck us, but the storm of fear hits hard and plays havoc with us. It makes the hands unsteady, the knees tremble, and the heart weak. It has blighted many fond hopes and killed many worthy endeavors. It has blocked spiritual, social, and business progress. Many persons with considerable ability and many other admirable qualities have failed because they lacked this one necessary trait to succeed — courage. Their fears defeated them. This was the downfall of the one-talent man in the parable. He said, "I was afraid, and went and hid thy talent in the earth" (Matthew 25:25). The world belongs to those who are not afraid to possess it.

• *The cause of our fears is usually imaginary instead of real.* Oftentimes we are frightened by false alarms. The past teaches us that most things we feared were only the creations of our own fearful mind. We have scared ourselves! We have been afraid of the darkness when in reality the sun was shining. The thing we feared was only a passing

◆

shadow from a fast-moving cloud.

Though life is made up of mere bubbles
'Tis better than many aver,
For while we've a whole lot of troubles
The most of them never occur.

— NIXON WATERMANN

• *Whatever our state is, life should be lived realistically and courageously.* Even real problems are not too hard, if we have the courage to face them. Perhaps you have seen a child with a cut finger, holding it off at a distance, with head turned, afraid to look at it. But when he got the courage to face his little difficulty and permit treatment, then it was not so terrible. Maybe this is one reason we grow less afraid as we grow older — at least, those of us who have borne many sorrows and faced many trials. We have found all our problems solvable, one way or another, when we looked them straight in the face and came to grips with them.

We have found that behind adversity's frown there is usually a sweet smile. Some of our cares in life have become quite familiar to us and our bearing them has become somewhat natural — not that the cares have become lighter but that we ourselves have become stronger. Trials which break some people strengthen others, depending upon the stuff that is in them. We have many blessings which never would have come to us, except through

◆

adversity. And we are quick to acknowledge that it is better to have trouble and blessing together than it is to be denied them both. Shakespeare truthfully expressed it: "Sweet are the uses of adversity."

> *The good are better made by ill,*
> *As odors crushed are sweeter still.*
>
> — SAMUEL ROGERS

> *Our toil is sweet with thankfulness,*
> *Our burden is our boon;*
> *The curse of earth's gray morning is*
> *The blessing of its noon.*
>
> — JOHN GREENLEAF WHITTIER

The years have taught us that distress is often a blessing in disguise. This lesson gives us heart to keep up the fight. The older call back to the younger: "Come on! All is well!"

• *Both courage and fear are affairs of the heart.* Each is an inward condition that controls outward behavior in times of trial, peril, and difficulty. So if we would cure ourselves of fear, we must look within ourselves. Outside forces may give us temporary relief, but definitely no cure. Fear is produced by a cause; and when that cause is removed, courage will fill the heart instead. Here are some causes of fear:

1) With some, fear is the by-product of selfishness. Self-interest may cause a person to be so

◆

concerned with what is affecting him that fear grips and controls him. Fear increases with our self-regard. An inflated balloon is more vulnerable than one not blown up. Likewise, the more one becomes blown up with self-love the larger target he becomes for fear to hit him. Self-centeredness with all its idle pre-occupation is a fountainhead of fear. To overcome it, we must find some interest which is so great and worthwhile that it causes us to lose ourselves in the bigger issue.

We have a forceful example of this in the life of the apostle Paul. He knew that bonds and afflictions awaited him. But he faced them unafraid, because he counted not his life dear unto himself (Acts 20:22-24). In losing his life, he found it.

2) Fear also springs from doubt. Doubt has fear; faith has courage. Someone wrote: "Fear knocked at the door. Faith opened it. No one was there." Faith drives away fear. Blessed is the person who believes in God, himself, and others. Many people are shot through and through with an inferiority complex which stems from their little faith in themselves. They believe their doubts and doubt their beliefs. They doubt that they can measure up to what society demands of them. Quit doubting yourself. Just trust in the Lord and do the best you can — and let the results take care of themselves. No person succeeds at everything all the time. No ball player knocks a home run every time he goes to bat — and the world does not expect it.

The best way to believe in self is first to believe

◆

in God. As faith in God increases, faith in self also increases; and as faith increases, fear decreases. One of the world's greatest leaders overcame fear through faith. This was Moses. The Bible says, "By faith he forsook Egypt, not fearing the wrath of the king."

Have faith, and thy faith shall sustain thee;
Permit not suspicion and care
With invisible bonds to acclaim thee
But bear what God gives thee to bear.

By his spirit supported and gladdened,
Be ne'er by forebodings deterred;
But think how oft hearts have been saddened
By fear of what never occurred.

— Charles Swain

No coward soul is mine
No trembler in the world's storm-trouble sphere.
I see heaven's glories shine,
And Faith shines equal, arming me from Fear.

— Bronte

3) "Conscience doth make cowards of us all." An accusing conscience runs wild with imagination. As an extreme example, it is said that Bessus, a Grecian, pulled down the bird's nests about his house because he stated that the birds never ceased to accuse him of the murder of his father. The

◆

singing of the little birds were songs of peace; but to this fearful man with a gnawing conscience they were sounds of condemnation.

> *It is the nature and quality of a guilty conscience to flee and be terrified, even when all is well, and when prosperity abounds, and to change such prosperity into danger.*
> — MARTIN LUTHER

Many are afraid because a condemning conscience rises like a ghost in the dark to scare them. Their strength has been divided between two opposing and pulling powers within themselves — good and evil. Self-respect, true manliness, and an approving conscience will give one power to face the world, sin, and the devil. Keep your conscience clear, and it will be a source of courage.

4) Fear also arises from a sense of loneliness. The solitary soul is more easily scared. The presence of others gives us courage. A soldier may be afraid to make a dangerous mission alone, but fight bravely with mates at his side. The thought of dying alone terrifies him, but he can make the supreme sacrifice in the presence of others without a whimper of fear.

No one is alone when God is with him. The presence and companionship of God drives away fear. A little child is afraid in the dark, but only when the mother is away. When the mother's hand

◆

is laid on the child's head, courage enters that little one's heart. God's presence in life is a safeguard against fear, an assurance against evil, and an inspiration to courage.

The Bible says: "Fear thou not; for I am with thee; be not dismayed; for I am thy God: I will strengthen thee; yea, I will help thee" (Isaiah 41:10). The same God who spoke these words to Israel still lives. We are not afraid, because He marches by our side.

> *Courage, brother! do not stumble,*
> *Though thy path be dark as night;*
> *There's a star to guide the humble;*
> *Trust in God and do the Right.*
>
> — MACLEOD

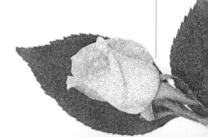

CHAPTER TEN

'I Will Fear No Evil"

As a continuation of the theme in the previous chapter, we meditate upon these words, "I will fear no evil" (Psalms 23:4). They were spoken by David, but were meant to be an inspiration to all of us. "I will fear no evil" — no past, present, nor future evil; no imaginary or real evil; "for thou art with me."

But we unnecessarily keep on being scared. Here are some of our most common fears:

• *Some fear sickness.* But fearing it is the best way to develop it. Do not fear sickness; the ailment you fear may never come. If it does come, it may be a blessing in disguise.

Both the well and the sick have reason to hope for a longer life. Every day we learn more about the things given by the gracious God to cure us of our ailments. And every day we learn more about how

◆

to preserve health. Consequently, the span of life is being lengthened. We fear what we think may interfere with our progress and happiness. Sickness does not necessarily have to hinder either. Some of the happiest people we know have been afflicted with ill health for many years. Some of the world's most successful people worked their way up in spite of physical handicaps. This was true of Robert Louis Stevenson. He never saw a well day in his life. But he left to the world a great legacy of literature. Examples could be multiplied. Strength of will lifted them above their afflictions. They did not give up! Neither were they afraid!

After all, the best health is the ability to live in bad health undaunted and unafraid.

Our greatest problem is not how to add years to life, but how to add life to years. This way, we can live while we live. To do this, we must not be afraid!

• *Some fear that they may not have enough material things in life.* These fearful people need to realize that we can eat only one meal at a time, wear only one suit at a time, and occupy only one room at a time. Really, we do not need very much. We forget that life is more than meat and the body is more than raiment. Christ pointed to the birds and said to a people who felt their insecurity, "Your heavenly Father feedeth them. Are ye not much better than they?" If a sparrow cannot fly through the heavens without attracting His attention, surely

◆

the needs of His people cannot go unnoticed.

The Sparrow

I am only a little sparrow,
A bird of low degree;
My life is of little value,
But the dear Lord cares for me.

If my meal is sometimes scanty,
Close picking makes it sweet;
I have always enough to feed me,
And "life is more than meat."

Though small, we are not forgotten;
Though weak we are never afraid;
For we know that the dear Lord keepeth
The life of the creatures he made.

God has given us brain and brawn, summer and winter, sunshine and rain, sprouting and harvest. His blessings are too numerous for us to fear starvation. What we need to do is to work, use His blessings, and trustingly pray, "Give us this day our daily bread," and we shall have enough. We know that we shall, for He has promised.

• *Others fear failure in life.* But what is success? This depends entirely upon the gauges we use. All God expects is that we do our best. He who

◆

does much — comparatively speaking — with little has succeeded, while he who has done little — comparatively speaking — with much has failed. It is not how much we do, but how much we do with what we have that spells success. The person who does his best should never fear failure; for he is a success.

> *The world is wide*
> *In time and tide,*
> *And God is guide;*
> *Then do not hurry.*
> *That man is blest*
> *Who does his best*
> *And leaves the rest;*
> *Then do not worry.*
> — CHARLES F. DEEMS

Success cannot be measured in terms of a few "flash-in-the-pan" achievements. True success is to fear God and keep His commandments (Ecclesiastes 12:1). Hence, success cannot be fully determined until the end of life.

> *Let no one till his death*
> *Be called unhappy. Measure not the work*
> *Until the day's out and the labor done;*
> *Then bring your gauges.*
> — ELIZABETH BARRETT BROWNING

◆

- *Others fear society.* They fear what others may think, feel, and say. They live in fear that their dress, automobile, home, furniture, speech, and job may not be good enough to please a critical and heartless world. This is truly a foolish fear. What difference does it make how others feel, if we do not hurt them! They are not our standard. They have no right to run our lives. They have all they can do to run their own. Furthermore, it is futile to try to please everybody. No one can do it. Not even Jesus Christ could. So there is but one intelligent thing to do; please God, live your own life, run your own business, and let others think what they will. You will be surprised how much better you will feel and how much more you will be appreciated. There is entirely too much tendency to put everybody in the same mold of public opinion. Be yourself!

If you are having trouble overcoming this fear, then learn well these verses from the Bible and quote them often:

The Lord is my helper, and I will not fear what man shall do unto me.
— HEBREWS 13:6

The Lord is on my side; I will not fear: what can man do unto me?
— PSALMS 118:6

◆

• *Some fear old age.* How useless! For no one has the power to hold back the hands of the clock of life. Whether we like it or not, they just keep on turning at the same speed. Regardless of age, life is still what we make it. There is nothing to fear in old age when we realize that our accomplishments and abilities need not necessarily decline with accumulation of years. There is a world of evidence to teach us this is right. For instance: Commodore Vanderbilt between 70 and 83 added about 100 millions to his fortune. Verdi at 74 produced his masterpiece, "Othello"; at 80, "Falstaff," and at 85, the famous "Ave Maria." Cato at 80 began the study of Greek. When asked why he began the study of such a difficult language so late in life, he replied, "Because I didn't start sooner." Tennyson at 83 wrote "Crossing the Bar."

It is never too late!

Old age can be the happiest and most fruitful years of life. By virtue of experience, the aged should be able to give more to life and thus get more from it. Age is grossly misunderstood! These poetic words shed light on what it actually is:

An age so blest that, by its side
Youth seems the waste instead.

— ROBERT BROWNING

◆

For what is age but youth's full bloom
A riper, more transcendent youth?
A weight of gold is never old.

Even though we are old in years we can still be young in heart. There is nothing to fear in age. We can so live that our last years will be our best. Praying the beautiful thoughts written by John Greenleaf Whittier will enrich our riper years:

Fill, brief or long, my granted years
Of life with love to thee and man;
Strike when thou wilt, the hour of rest,
But let my last days be my best.

• *Many fear death.* Death was designed, however, as one of our most needed blessings. The Bible says, "Precious in the sight of Jehovah is the death of his saints." It was not good for man to live forever in a world of sin, rebellion, and strife. So God arranged for the dissolution of flesh and spirit which is called death. God intended for death to serve as an exit to this world and an entrance to another world.

In God's plan of things, death is necessary because "flesh and blood cannot inherit the kingdom of God." These bodies of flesh and blood are not suited to an eternal habitation. We have to lay them aside that our souls may be clothed with new bodies "like unto His glorious body."

◆

In this present world, we must have death in order to have life. Suppose no one should ever die — many births but no deaths — life would soon become unbearable. Think how terrible it would be if suffering people could not die. Death was designed to be gain. The Bible says, "To live is Christ and to die is gain." This solves the problem of life, and then there is no problem to death. Take care of life, and death will take care of itself. Then you can say in the comforting language of David in the Twenty-Third Psalm: "Yea, though I walk through the valley of the shadow of death, I will fear no evil: for thou art with me." There is courage to be gained in repeating again and again this verse from the Bible. Make it one of your rules of life.

So live that when thy summons comes to join
The innumerable caravan which moves
To that mysterious realm where each shall take
His chamber in the silent halls of death,
Thou go not like the quarry slave at night
Scourged to his dungeon; but, sustained and
*   soothed*
By an unfaltering trust, approach thy grave
Like one who wraps the drapery of his couch
About him and lies down to pleasant dreams.

— *Thanatopsis*,
William Cullen Bryant

◆

The phrase "fear not" occurs eighty-one times in the Bible. God meant for His people to be unafraid. We would expect that of Him since He knows no fears. It is His will that we do our best in life, and this is impossible if we are fearful. Tell yourself there is nothing to fear but God, and that this fear is different, a fear joined with love and hope like a son respects his father. It can be summed up in one statement: the person who fears God has no cause for any other fear.

CHAPTER ELEVEN

"Closer Than a Brother"

*T*he Bible says, "There is a friend that sticketh closer than a brother" (Proverbs 18:24). This is a great tribute to true friendship. A brother is not always a friend. The relationship of natural brothers may become unglued. Brothers are a matter of flesh and blood where there may or may not be love and loyalty. But friendship is a matter of the heart and true friendship is the feeling of a true heart. False hearts can be brothers, but not true friends.

• *Friendship has been defined in many beautiful terms.* Even though the terminology has varied, the thought has remained uniform. The world is agreed on the meaning of friendship and the use of it. Cicero stated, "Friendship is the only thing in the world concerning the use of which all mankind are agreed."

At a social function the conversation drifted to the subject of friendship, and the following apt and interesting definitions were given:

An athlete said, "In my opinion, a friend is a balancing-pole that enables us to walk the tight-rope of life without falling."

A physician stated, "I believe a friend may be likened to a soft bandage and a soothing ointment for the cuts and bruises of life."

"A friend is a golden link in the chain of life," said a jeweler.

A botanist gave this view: "A friend is a vine that clings to us and hides the discrepancies and rough places of life." And a florist added, "And the greater the ruin, the closer such a friend clings."

A woman in mourning joined in: "A friend is the one who comes in when the whole world goes out."

"The best friend of all," said a white-haired man of eighty-six, "is Jesus, who said, 'Greater love hath no man than this, that a man lay down his life for his friends'."

• *The Bible says: "A man that hath friends must show himself friendly."* This is an unalterable rule of life. Friendship begets friendship, and friendship requires friendship as its reciprocation. If we do not maintain a friendly deportment, we cannot expect to keep our friends. Friendship is a beautiful flower in life's garden that requires cultivation to make it grow. "Real friendship...never thrives unless ingrafted upon a stock of known and

reciprocal merit," said Lord Chesterfield. This is what makes friendship so sweet — it is so needful.

A deaf man and a blind man found a precious friendship in conversing with each other by using the Morse code by means of a unique system of telegraph instruments. An electric bulb showed the flashes for the deaf one, and the blind man heard the ticks from the sounder.

So it is with the whole human family. What one lacks, another possesses. We possess many things in common, but no person is so endowed as to need no help from others. Thus we find in others strength for our weaknesses, and they in turn find in us good measure for their own insufficiency. This is what makes friendship so helpful. It is so valuable that he who has friends is rich.

• *A friend is a stand-by for adversity.* The Bible says, "A friend loveth at all times, and a brother is born for adversity" (Proverbs 17:17). Adversity is the power that separates true friends from designing flatterers.

The Shadow once said to the Body: "You don't have another friend like me. I follow you in sunlight and in moonlight. I never forsake you."

"That is true," replied the Body, "You do go with me in sunlight and in moonlight. But where are you when neither the sun nor the moon shines upon me? Then you forsake me."

The true friend is faithful in adversity and abides with us in all kinds of weather day or night. He is no fair-weather shadow.

◆

Life is filled with adversity. On the highway of life we often come to the sign, "Detour"! After many miles of smooth traveling, we suddenly come upon the barrier with the sign, "Detour"! We are almost tempted to run the barrier. But to do so is to risk danger and defeat. So better judgment compels us to turn back. We are forced to leave the fine smooth road for the rough and dusty way, and our traveling is toilsome and difficult. Sometimes life's detour calls for us to go to the hospital for a stay, to the cemetery where we give up a loved one, to a loss of job status, to some misunderstanding that brings us persecution, to some failure that has lowered our spirits, or to some foolish act that shames us.

But whatever the detour may be, our friends travel with us to help us over the roughest places. They write us. They visit us. They counsel us. They pray for us. They stick closer than a brother. Truly "a friend is born for adversity."

 • *The four greatest friends of the Bible are the Lord, Abraham, Jonathan, and Onesiphorus.*

In speaking of the Lord, the Bible says, "Greater love hath no man than this, that a man lay down his life for his friends" (John 15:13). This is a severe test of friendship. A friendship unwilling to sacrifice is no friendship at all. Jesus more than passed the test — He sacrificed life, and that sacrifice was for His enemies as well as for His friends. What a friend.

◆

What a friend we have in Jesus,
All our sins and griefs to bear.

Abraham has the distinction of being the only person directly mentioned in the Bible as the friend of God. "And the Scripture was fulfilled which saith, Abraham believed God, and it was imputed unto him for righteousness: and he was called the friend of God" (James 2:23). What a beautiful tribute to a noble life. No man was ever paid a finer compliment. He made mistakes, yes, but the general tenor of his life was one of friendship with God. We too can be friends of the Lord, and many are. He said, "Ye are my friends, if ye do whatsoever I command you" (John 15:13).

Jonathan was David's unfaltering friend. He is the greatest human friend of the Old Testament. When David's needs were the greatest, when he was pursued day and night by the undying hatred and relentless jealousy of King Saul, he found strength in his noble friendship with Jonathan. The Bible says Jonathan "strengthened his hand in the Lord." Friends strengthen our hands and hold them up. That is natural, just as natural as it is for the world to keep on turning. As the clouds of adversity became darker, this friendship became brighter — but this is natural too. The poets have written many odes to friends, but David's ode to Jonathan is the tenderest and most expressive of them all.

Onesiphorus' friendship to the apostle Paul has handed him down to immortality. Wherever and whenever men read the New Testament, they read of Onesiphorus' friendship to Paul which chains could not break. Paul, in speaking of him, says, "He oft refreshed me, and was not ashamed of my chain" (II Timothy 1:16). Paul was in prison. Many of his friends were afraid and ashamed. The world's contempt and scorn, hatred and danger, the probability of being next in a blood purge of Christians, could not break his friendship. And when he died, a fitting epitaph to be engraved on his tomb would have been: "A friend of Paul — a friend that sticketh closer than a brother." But regardless of what may be written on our tomb-stones, we can write on our hearts the meaning of friendship — for friendship is a state of the heart.

• Being a friend includes many things. What does friendship mean to you? All of us have friends who enrich and beautify our lives. Perhaps one of the most expressive descriptions of true friendship is that written a few years ago:

> *I love you not only for what you are, but for*
> *what I am when I am with you.*
> *I love you not only for what you are making of*
> *yourself, but for what you are making of me.*
> *I love you for that part of me that you bring*
> *out.*
> *I love you for putting your hand into my*
> *heaped-up heart, and passing over all the*
> *foolish, and frivolous, and weak things that*

◆

you cannot help dimly seeing there,
for drawing out into the light all the
beautiful and radiant qualities that no one
else has looked quite deep enough to find.
I love you for ignoring the possibility of the
fool in me and laying hold of the possibility
of good.
I love you for closing your ears to the discords
in me, and for adding to the harmony in
me by reverent listening.
I love you because you are helping me to make
the structure of my life not a tavern,
but a temple;
and the words of my every day not a reproach
but a song. You have done it just by being
yourself. Perhaps this is what being a friend
means after all.

— ROY CROFT

A Father's Prayer

*H*ere is a father's prayer for his son:

God in heaven, I as a humble, earthly father, beseech thee, the great Heavenly Father, to bless my son, flesh of my flesh, and bone of my bone. Raise him, Oh God, to be strong enough to know when he is weak...and weak enough to know that he needs strength...and brave enough to face fear within himself...gentle and humble in victory... courageous and noble in defeat...a son whose foundation for learning is a knowledge of God and a knowledge of himself.

My son...may he have clean hands and a pure heart...a goal high enough to challenge the best within him. A son who will master self-control before he seeks to control others. One who will learn to laugh without forgetting how to weep, and will know when to do each. A son who will

◆

enhance his future by profiting from his past.

Spare him not from life's battles, but make him strong enough for the fight. I ask not that he travel the paths of least resistance, the ways of idleness, ease, and comfort, but that his pathway be so wrought with stress and difficulties that it will make him a man. May there be just enough opposing winds to lift him high.

I pray that he may learn to stand on his own feet, yet be compassionate toward those who fall. Let him learn to be serious without taking himself too seriously...to work and to work hard, but to know when to rest. Rear him to see life as a privilege and not as a prosecution. May he put much into life that he may get much from it. May he have humility in honor, simplicity in greatness, and meekness in strength...a son who will be a friend to God, a friend to humanity, and a friend to himself. And I shall be grateful forever and rejoice in the life of my son. In the name of Christ, thy Son. Amen.